SCARS
OF THE
DESERT
ROSE

Ahmed
Mustafa

Hidayah
Publishers

Scars of the Desert Rose

ISBN (Paperback): 978-1-998843-49-7

Printed in the United States of America

CONTENTS

Preface

My dear friend, I see you. I see the pain you carry, the invisible scars of trauma, abuse, or loss that ache within your heart. I know the feeling of being shattered, of wondering if the pieces of your life can ever be put back together again. You've walked through a fire, and the path has been arduous. But hey, you're not alone, and there is hope, even if it's hard to see right now. Your resilience has brought you this far, and that same strength will carry you forward.

Perhaps, like many who have experienced deep suffering, you've found solace in Rumi's poetry. His words, like a gentle hand reaching out in the darkness, offer a glimpse of a different path, a way to transform pain into wisdom, and wounds into sources of light. This book is an extension of that hand, offering companionship in your process of healing, guided by the wisdom of Rumi and grounded in practical tools to help you reclaim your life.

I know the struggles you face – the flashbacks that steal your peace, the nightmares that haunt your sleep, the emotional pain that can feel overwhelming at times. Perhaps you find it hard to trust, to build healthy relationships, or to quiet the inner critic that whispers of shame and unworthiness. These are the heavy burdens carried by a heart that has been deeply wounded. But they are burdens you no longer have to bear alone.

Consider this book a haven, a compassionate space where your pain is acknowledged, your struggles are validated, and your deep desire for healing is honored. Within these pages, we'll navigate a course designed specifically for those who have faced the fire of trauma and emerged, scarred but not broken, yearning to reclaim their lives and find lasting peace.

This book won't offer quick fixes or easy answers, but it will offer you a gentle, guiding hand and practical tools to help you navigate the complexities of healing. Think of it as a process of discovery. We'll learn how to cultivate self-compassion, quieting that harsh inner critic and replacing it with a voice of kindness. We'll explore how to rebuild trust, both in yourself and others, learning to recognize those who are truly worthy of your trust, and how to create healthy boundaries to protect your heart. We'll also discover the freedom that forgiveness brings, releasing the weight of resentment and opening your heart to a new chapter of peace and joy. And most importantly, we'll rediscover your true self, reconnecting with the inner strength, resilience, and the inherent worthiness that has always been within you, waiting to shine.

This is a path of courage, vulnerability, and deep inner work. But it is also a path that leads to sheer healing, lasting peace, and the reclamation of a life filled with joy, purpose, and authentic connection. It is a journey of transforming your deepest wounds into your greatest sources of strength. The journey awaits, and you are ready to begin.

Welcome, brave and beautiful soul. Let's walk this path together.

- Ahmed Mustafa

Chapter 1

WOUNDS & WISDOM

Logs of wood would not be duly shaped

Did not the carpenter plan outline and detail.

If vile base copper were not mingled,

How could the alchemist show his skill?

Defects are the mirrors of the attributes of Beauty,

The base is the mirror of the High and Glorious One,

Because one contrary shows forth its contrary,

As honey's sweetness is shown by vinegar's sourness.

Whoso recognizes and confesses his own defects

Is hastening in the way that leads to perfection!

– Rumi

My friend, let these words of Rumi sink deep into your heart. He speaks of a truth that many of us spend our lives running from: that our imperfections, those very things we try to hide or fix, are essential to our growth and beauty. Think of the carpenter and the alchemist—they don't work with flawless materials, do they? No, they take the raw, the imperfect, and through their skill, reveal its hidden potential. You, too, are like that raw material, full of potential, waiting to be unlocked. The cracks, the wounds, the things you might see as flaws—these are not signs of weakness, but places where your strength and resilience can shine through. This chapter is about valuing that journey, about understanding that the path to wholeness isn't about becoming perfect, but about accepting all of yourself, especially the parts that feel broken or incomplete. Trust me, it is in those very imperfections that your unique beauty lies, waiting to be discovered. Just as contrasting flavors bring out the best in each other, your vulnerabilities, when acknowledged, can illuminate the brilliance of your spirit. Let's walk this path together and uncover the incredible strength and beauty that resides within you.

We all have our hurts. Some are easy to see. Maybe you've got a scar on your knee from falling off your bike or a story about how you got that mark above your eye. But many are invisible. The pain, the things that make us feel small or unseen, they are hidden deep down where we don't have to look at them. We carry them around like secrets, tucked away in our hearts. These are often from a long time ago, maybe when we were little. They shape us. They shape the way we act, how we feel about ourselves, and how we move through the world. This whole chapter is about saying "hello" to those hurts. It's about realizing how they've changed you and seeing the beauty in being a little imperfect. Knowing that the cracks in who you are, aren't weaknesses. They are, as the great poet said, how the light gets in.

A lot of us are walking around with hurts that we don't even fully understand. They're like old injuries that didn't quite heal right. You know, like when you sprain your ankle, and it still aches sometimes, even years later? You learn to walk differently, to favor that ankle, but the pain is still there, affecting how you move. Emotional wounds can be like that. They can come from things that happened when you were a kid, hard times in relationships, losing someone you loved, being betrayed, or any tough thing life throws your way. These things can be really big and dramatic, or they can be small and sneaky. But they all leave a mark.

Maybe when you were growing up, you were always being criticized. Maybe your feelings were brushed off, or you were made to feel like you were never quite good enough. Maybe you went through a tough breakup or lost someone close to you, and it shattered your ability to trust. These things, especially when they happen when we're young, can really impact how we see ourselves. They can make us believe that we're not worthy, that we're unlovable, or that we don't belong.

I'd like to share a very beautiful verse from the Quran:

"Verily, with every hardship comes ease."

(Surah Ash-Sharh, 94:6)

This verse is a gentle reminder that there's a light at the end of the tunnel and hard times don't last forever. It's like a promise from the Divine that even when things are tough, there's hope. Challenges are a part of life, but they also bring opportunities for growth.

Now, let's take a moment to connect with those hidden hurts. Find a quiet place where you can sit comfortably. Close your eyes if you feel comfortable doing so.

1. **Take a few deep breaths.** Inhale slowly and deeply, and exhale slowly. Let your body relax with each breath.

2. **Now, gently scan your body. Are there any places that feel particularly heavy or achy?** Maybe your chest feels tight, or your stomach feels like it's in knots.

3. **What feeling might be associated with that place?** Is it sadness? Fear? Anger? Loneliness? Just acknowledge the feeling without judgment.

4. **Can you think of a time in your past, maybe from your childhood, when you felt that same feeling?** Don't force it, just let a memory gently surface if it's ready.

5. **Sit with that memory for a few moments.** Observe it like you're watching a movie, without getting too caught up in the details.

6. **Now, take another deep breath and remind yourself that you are safe in this present moment.** That was then, and this is now.

7. **When you're ready, slowly open your eyes.**

This exercise is just a starting point. It's a way to acknowledge those hidden hurts and recognizing how they might still be affecting you today. You don't have to have all the answers right now. The important thing is to start paying attention, to start listening to the whispers of your body and your heart.

Mind-Body Connection

Emotional pain is not solely in your mind; it is stored within your body as well. When you experience something deeply challenging, such as trauma, it doesn't just stay in your thoughts; it alters your body too. As Bessel van der Kolk explored in "The Body Keeps the Score," these experiences change both our bodies and brains, affecting our ability to feel joy, connect with others, manage emotions, and trust.

Consider how fear triggers survival mode. Your heart races, muscles tense, and you breathe rapidly as your body prepares to fight, flee, or freeze. This is a normal response, but when these experiences persist or become overwhelming, these responses can become stuck, making your body react as if the danger is still present. This can manifest in physical symptoms like pain, anxiety, depression, sleep problems, and stomach issues—your body remembering the trauma, even when your mind pushes it away.

The world often tells us we need to be perfect, equating flawlessness with worthiness. We hide our flaws, hurts, and vulnerabilities, but this act is draining. It requires considerable energy to maintain a facade. Dealing with trauma and emotional wounds takes strength, especially when managing difficult emotions. It is about learning healthy coping strategies and controlling reactions, rather than letting emotions control you.

The Beauty of Our Wounds

Kintsugi, the Japanese art of repairing broken pottery with gold, offers a powerful metaphor for our own healing. Instead of hiding the cracks, Kintsugi artists highlight them, making them a special part of the object's beauty. The mended piece becomes more valuable, unique, and beautiful than before it was broken. This is a great way to think about our own healing. Our hurts, our scars, our imperfections—they don't make us less valuable or less beautiful. They're part of our story. They show how strong we are, how resilient we are, and how we can heal. When we accept our imperfections, when we let ourselves be seen in our brokenness, we make room for something new to grow.

Healing begins by telling your story, giving voice to the pain you've carried in silence. Understanding that your experiences, no matter how difficult, have shaped who you are today. This can be scary. It takes guts, and it means being vulnerable. You have to be willing to look at the parts of yourself that you might have been trying to avoid. But it's also freeing. When you tell your story, when you give a voice to your pain, you take away its power over you. You take back control of your own life.

In a world that's all about being perfect, loving your imperfections is a big deal. It's a way of saying,

> *"I love and accept myself, not in spite of my flaws, but because of them."*

Your imperfections are what make you human. They make you unique. They make you, you. It's about letting go of the need to be perfect, to have it all together, to always be strong. It's about letting yourself be vulnerable, be messy, be real. It's about showing up as your true self, with all the flaws, and knowing that you are enough. Think of a really old tree. It's not perfectly straight. It has knots and bumps, and its branches go in all different directions. But it's also strong. It's been through storms and It survived. And those imperfections are exactly what make it so special and so beautiful.

Healing from old hurts and accepting your imperfections is a process of learning about yourself and growing. We're all in this together, learning to accept our imperfections, heal our hurts, and become the best versions of ourselves. You're not defined by what's happened to you or by your imperfections. You're so much more than that. You're strong, you're resilient, and you're capable of amazing growth and change.

Exercise

Now, I want you to take the first step. Take a journal and write about a time that was hard for you. Don't overthink it. Don't worry about making it perfect or even coherent. Just let the words flow. Let your pain out onto the page. This is your first step in giving voice to your pain, in acknowledging your story, and in reclaiming your narrative. This is you, starting to let your light shine through the cracks.

Those cracks are, after all, what makes you unique. They are proof of your strength and your ability to heal. Own them. Let them be a reminder that even in the darkest of times, there is always light to be found. That light is within you, waiting to be discovered. It's the light of your true self, the light of your resilience, the light of your capacity to grow and heal. And it all starts with acknowledging those cracks, those imperfections, those wounds that have shaped you into the incredible person you are today.

Whoso recognizes and confesses his own defects

Is hastening in the way that leads to perfection!

～

Chapter 2

THE CLEANSING RAIN

I use the dust of my grief as salve for my eyes,

That my eyes, like seas, may teem with pearls.

The tears which are shed because of His chastening

Are very pearls, though men deem them mere tears.

Tis 'The Soul of souls' of whom I am making complaint;

Yet I do not complain; I merely state my case.

My heart says, "He has injured me,"

But I laugh at these pretended injuries.

— Rumi

Let's walk together into the heart of these verses, where Rumi offers us a thoughtful perspective on grief. He's offering us a view, one that sees it not as something to be feared or pushed away, but as a wise teacher in disguise. He speaks of tears as precious pearls, formed not from ease, but from the very pressure of loss and heartache. It is okay to feel pain. Don't fight the sadness. Don't be ashamed of your tears. There's a beautiful surrender in those verses, a willingness to simply 'state my case' to the heart of existence, acknowledging the pain without demanding answers. This chapter opens the door to a sacred space, where we give grief the freedom to voice itself through our tears. Together, we will explore how embracing sorrow, and allowing ourselves to feel it fully, can become a source of healing, a balm for the soul. Just as the ocean's depths hold treasures unseen on the surface, your tears, when honored, can reveal a wellspring of resilience, wisdom, and a deeper appreciation for life's fullness. Trust that grief, in its own time and way, can guide you toward inner peace and a richer understanding of yourself.

Grief is something we all go through. It's a natural response to losing something or someone important to us. That loss might be a loved one, a relationship, a dream, a job, or even a part of ourselves. But in our society, we often treat grief like it's something to be ashamed of, something to hide or hurry through. We're told to "be strong," to "move on," to "get over it." But grief doesn't work like that. It doesn't just disappear because we ignore it or try to push it down. When we don't deal with our grief, it can weigh us down. It's like carrying a heavy stone in your heart. It can manifest as anxiety, depression, anger, and even physical illness. It can cloud our thinking, hurt our relationships, and stop us from fully enjoying life. It's like trying to run a marathon with a backpack full of rocks. You might be able to do it for a while, but sooner or later, the weight will be too much to carry.

Tears, which are often seen as a sign of weakness, are actually a powerful balm for the pain of grief. They're your body's way of expressing what words can't. They're a language of the soul, a way of communicating the depth of your pain, your love, your longing. Think of your tears as a pressure valve. When the pressure inside gets too high, the valve releases, preventing an explosion. In the same way, when the emotional pressure of grief builds up, tears provide a much-needed outlet. They let us release some of that pent-up emotion, cleansing our hearts and minds. And science backs this up. Studies have shown that emotional tears contain stress hormones and other toxins. Crying literally helps to get rid of these harmful substances from your body. It is a detox for the soul, a natural cleansing process we should welcome rather than suppress. They wash away the pain of the past, making space for new life to emerge. They nourish the garden of your soul, helping it to bloom again, even after the hardest of times.

Despite the natural role of tears in the grieving process, there's often a stigma attached to them. Many of us have been taught, in one way or another, that crying is something to be avoided, that it's a sign of weakness or a lack of control. These societal messages can be particularly strong for some, but they affect all of us to some degree. We learn to suppress our tears, to hold them back, to present a stoic facade to the world, even when we're hurting inside. This pressure to hide our grief can be really damaging. It leads to a buildup of unexpressed emotions that can harm our mental and physical health.

We must break the silence surrounding grief and cultivate a culture where vulnerability is valued and tears are recognized as a sign of strength, not weakness. It's time to see that grieving is a natural, healthy, and necessary part of being human. We're not meant to keep it all bottled up inside. It's time to challenge those old beliefs that tell us to hide our tears, to "suck it up," or to "just get over it." Those messages are not only unhelpful, they're harmful. They prevent us from experiencing the healing power of grief, from allowing ourselves to fully process our loss and move towards a place of greater peace and acceptance.

Healing from grief involves making space for it, and letting yourself feel all the emotions that come with loss. This can be hard and painful, but it's essential for your well-being. It's about permitting yourself to grieve, to mourn, to feel the pain without judgment or shame.

Acknowledge your loss. Know that you've experienced a loss and that it's okay to grieve. Don't try to downplay or deny your pain.

Let yourself feel. Give yourself permission to feel all the emotions that come up, even the tough ones like anger, sadness, guilt, and fear. Don't try to push them away or avoid them.

Find healthy ways to express your emotions. This could be talking to a trusted friend or family member, writing in a journal, making art, spending time in nature, or exercising.

Create rituals. Rituals can be a powerful way to honor your loss and process your grief. This could be lighting a candle, writing a letter to the person you've lost, or making a memory box.

Seek support. Don't be afraid to ask for help. Talk to a therapist, join a support group, or connect with others who have gone through similar losses.

The Quran says,

"And We will surely test you with something of fear and hunger and a loss of wealth and lives and fruits, but give good news to those who patiently endure."

(Surah Al-Baqarah, 2:155)

This verse reminds us that going through tough times, including grief, is a normal part of life. It's a test, but it also says that those who are patient and endure will receive good news. This can be comforting when you're grieving, knowing that you're not alone and that there's hope for healing.

Exercise

This week, commit to creating space for grief in one of the ways we discussed. It could be starting a journal, talking to a friend, or creating a small ritual to honor your loss. Pick something that feels right for you and commit to doing it. This is about action, not just contemplation; it's time to actively begin healing.

The Pearls of Grief

Consider grief not as merely something to endure, but as an experience that holds hidden treasures waiting to be discovered. I'm talking about those pearls of wisdom, formed in the very depths of sorrow. Each loss, each heartbreak, carries within it a lesson, a deeper understanding of yourself and this precious life we live. When you allow yourself to truly feel your grief, to sit with the pain instead of running from it, you create space for these pearls to surface. They might be hard to see at first, hidden behind the tears and the rawness of loss, but trust me, they are there, waiting to be found.

These pearls take many forms, one might whisper to you about the fragility of life, urging you to cherish every moment and to love fiercely while you can. Another might reveal a strength within you that you never knew existed, a resilience formed in the fire of loss. Yet another might open your heart to a deeper compassion for others who are hurting. And just like the pearl takes time to form, layer upon layer, these lessons take time to reveal themselves. Be patient with yourself.

Your tears are not a sign of weakness; They are proof of your love, a reflection of the depth of connection you shared. They show that something truly mattered. Don't be afraid to reach out for support, to lean on loved ones, friends, or your community. The strength that brought you to this point is still inside you, ready to be found again. Don't forget that.

Listen to the wisdom of Imam Ali,

"The worldly people attach great importance to the death of their bodies, but they themselves attach much greater importance to the death of hearts of the living." (From Part Three, The Spiritual Experience, Nahjul-Balagha)

This reminds us that the true tragedy is not the loss of the physical, but the loss of our spiritual heart. Grief, when honored, can prevent that very loss. It can awaken you to what truly matters, to the core of your being. It can draw you closer to your values, to the people you love, and to the Divine. The pain, though difficult, can become a refining fire, purifying your heart and guiding you toward a life of greater meaning.

So, let your tears flow. And as they do, be open to the pearls of wisdom that emerge from the depths. They are the treasures that will light your way long after the initial darkness of grief begins to fade. These pearls are the legacy of love, a reminder that even in loss, there is beauty, there is growth, and there is always, always hope.

Key Takeaways:

- Grief is a journey, a process, a path to healing. It's not about "getting over" your loss, but about learning to live with it, to integrate it into your life in a way that allows you to keep growing and finding joy.

- Value the unique, cleansing power of your tears. Tears are not something to be ashamed of, but a natural and necessary part of that journey. They are a language of the soul, a way of expressing the depth of your love and your pain. Let them cleanse your heart and make way for new growth. They are a detox for your soul, a way to release the pain and make space for healing.

- Know that you're not alone. Even when things are at their worst, there's always hope, a light that shines through the cracks of your heart, a light that can guide you on your path to healing.

The tears which are shed because of His chastening

Are very pearls, though men deem them mere tears.

∼

Chapter 3

THE LIGHTER PATH

His bitters are very sweets to my soul,

My sad heart is a lively sacrifice to my Beloved.

I am enamoured of my own grief and pain,

For it makes me well-pleasing to my peerless King.

– Rumi

Rumi's words here might seem strange at first. How can pain be a good thing? But stay with me, he's pointing to something important. He's talking about changing how we see our past hurts. This chapter is about letting go of past wounds and finding freedom. Think of it like this: when you hold onto anger and resentment, it's like carrying a heavy weight. It drags you down and keeps you stuck in the past. Forgiveness is about putting down that weight. It doesn't mean saying that what happened was okay. It means choosing to release the hurt so that it no longer controls you. It is not about liking the pain, but about seeing it differently. Rumi suggests that even our deepest wounds, the "bitters" of our lives, can become a path toward healing and a deeper connection with something greater than ourselves. Forgiveness is the bridge that takes us from a place of pain to a place of freedom. It's a path, and while it may not always be easy, it's one worth walking. It's about freeing your heart, and that's what we'll explore here together.

This chapter is about comprehending the power of forgiveness, not to condone the actions of others, but to liberate ourselves. Forgiveness, especially after we've been deeply hurt, can feel like an impossible task. When we've been wronged, especially when that wrong has caused us deep pain, it's natural to feel anger, resentment, and even a desire for revenge. These feelings are like heavy chains, binding us to the past, and preventing us from moving forward. We replay the events in our minds, each time adding another link to the chain, another layer to the wall around our hearts.

Holding onto resentment is like drinking poison and expecting the other person to die. It doesn't harm the person who hurt you, but it eats away at you from the inside. It consumes your thoughts, steals your joy, and robs you of your peace. It's like living in a prison of your own making, where the bars are forged from bitterness and the locks are fastened with anger. Think of it this way: imagine carrying a heavy backpack filled with rocks. Each rock represents a hurt, a betrayal, a disappointment. As you walk through life, that backpack gets heavier and heavier, weighing you down, making it difficult to move forward. Forgiveness is like taking those rocks out of the backpack, one by one, and setting them down. It doesn't mean that what happened was okay. It doesn't mean you approve of the actions of those who hurt you. It simply means that you are choosing to release the burden, to free yourself from the weight of the past. This involves choosing to no longer let those hurts define us or control us.

Let's say someone borrowed your favorite book, a book you treasured, and they returned it damaged, with torn pages and a stained cover. You'd likely feel upset, maybe even angry. You might hold onto that anger, reminding yourself and maybe even them, about how careless they were. But holding onto that anger wouldn't fix the book, would it? It wouldn't undo the damage. It would only make you feel worse. Each time you saw the damaged book, the memory of your anger and disappointment would resurface. Forgiveness, in this case, wouldn't mean saying it was okay that they damaged your book. It would mean accepting that the damage is done and choosing to release the anger so you can move on. Maybe you'd ask them to replace the book. Maybe you wouldn't lend them anything again, but you wouldn't let the anger consume you. You would clean it the best you can and move on. Forgiveness is choosing to release the anger, for your own sake, so you can find peace.

There are many mistaken ideas about forgiveness that can make it seem like an impossible, even undesirable, task. Let's clear those up right now. Forgiving someone doesn't mean you are excusing their behavior or letting them off the hook. Forgiveness is about releasing yourself from the grip of anger and resentment, not about absolving the other person of responsibility. You don't have to forget what happened in order to forgive. In fact, trying to forget can often be counterproductive.

Forgiveness as Self-Love

Forgiveness is about acknowledging the pain, processing the emotions, and choosing to release the negative energy associated with the event. Forgiveness is an internal process; making up is an external one. You can forgive someone without ever having a relationship with them again. You can forgive them from afar, for your own sake, without ever interacting with them. Making up requires trust, and trust may not be possible or safe to rebuild in certain situations. You will want to proceed with caution, if at all, with this. Forgiveness is often a process, a journey. It may take time, and you may need to revisit it again and again. So be patient with yourself.

There's an interesting story of Imam Ali in Rumi's Masnavi which could be an inspiration for forgiveness. In the early days of Islam, Imam Ali, the Prophet Muhammad's (P.B.U.H) son-in-law and a formidable warrior, met an enemy soldier on the battlefield. Ali's skill was unmatched, and soon his opponent was at his mercy, kneeling before him with Ali's sword raised, ready to strike. In a final act of defiance, the soldier spat directly into Ali's face. Most would have reacted with immediate fury, but Ali, with a clarity that belied his warrior's strength, instantly lowered his sword and stepped back, sparing his enemy's life.

The soldier, stunned and confused, questioned Ali. He was perplexed as to why Ali had pulled back, to not carry out the execution when he had clearly won the battle. He asked, "What did you see in me? What suppressed your anger?"

Ali, in response, spoke not of the soldier's actions, but of his own internal state. He explained, "I only fight for God; I am His servant, not a puppet to my own anger. The sword in my hand is guided by His will, not by my whims. When you spat, you raised an issue that was about me, not about God. Had I acted then, I would have been fighting partly for God, and partly for my own ego. Anger, for most, makes them lose their heads, but for me, it is my slave. Patience has freed me from the yoke of anger. It is why I chose to withdraw."

Like Ali, we too are presented with moments where anger tempts us to react, to lash out, and sometimes to hold onto hurts that keep us shackled to the past. But true strength lies not in retaliation, but in recognizing the prison of our own making and choosing, instead, to unlock the door. Forgiveness is that key; it doesn't excuse the wrong, but it sets you free. It's a conscious act of releasing the burden of bitterness, of trading the weight of resentment for the lightness of peace. In forgiveness, we reclaim our power and become the masters of our own hearts once more.

Forgiveness is, ultimately, an act of self-love. It's about choosing to free yourself from the chains of the past so that you can live a more joyful and fulfilling life. It's about reclaiming your power and refusing to let the actions of others define you. When you forgive, you release the negative energy that has been holding you captive. You create space for healing, for growth, for love, and for joy. You open yourself up to new possibilities and new experiences. It's like opening a window in a stuffy room, letting in fresh air and sunlight.

The Quran says,

"The reward of an evil deed is its equivalent. But whoever pardons and seeks reconciliation, then their reward is with Allah. He certainly does not like the wrongdoers."

(Surah Ash-Shuraa, 42:40)

This verse acknowledges that it's natural to want to retaliate when we've been hurt. But it also says that forgiveness is better, and that those who forgive will be rewarded by Allah. It's a powerful reminder that forgiveness is not a sign of weakness, but of strength.

The Prophet Muhammad (peace be upon him) taught,

"If a person forgives someone who wronged them, seeking only Allah's pleasure, Allah will elevate their honor and status." (Sahih at-Targhib, 2426)

Forgiving is not easy. It can be a long and challenging process, especially when the wounds are deep. Yet, it is a path worth walking.

Acknowledge your pain. Allow yourself to feel the full range of emotions associated with the hurt or betrayal. Don't try to suppress or deny your feelings.

Understand your story. Reflect on what happened and how it impacted you. Writing in a journal can be a helpful tool for this process. Try to understand the other person's perspective, but don't excuse their behavior. Make a conscious decision to forgive.

Forgiveness is a choice. It's a decision to release the negative energy and move towards healing. Be kind to yourself throughout this process. Healing takes time.

Set healthy boundaries. Forgiveness doesn't mean you have to tolerate further abuse or disrespect. Set boundaries to protect yourself from future harm. Instead of dwelling on the past, focus your energy on the present moment.

Engage in activities that bring you joy and peace. Talk to a trusted friend, family member, or therapist. Consider joining a support group for people who have experienced similar traumas. Focusing on what you're grateful for can help shift your perspective and promote healing. Forgiveness is for your benefit. It sets you free from the grip of anger and resentment.

Exercise

Take out your journal and write down the name of one person you need to forgive. This could be someone who has hurt you deeply, or it could be yourself. Now, write down one reason why you want to forgive this person. Focus on your healing and liberation; not justifying their actions. Keep this journal entry somewhere safe, and revisit it as you continue on your forgiveness journey.

Often, the hardest person to forgive is ourselves. We carry guilt and shame for things we've done or things we think we should have done differently. We replay our mistakes in our minds, beating ourselves up over and over again. But self-forgiveness is essential for healing. It's about acknowledging your mistakes, learning from them, and then letting them go. Know that you are a human like everybody else, that you are imperfect, and that you are worthy of love and compassion, even if you mess up sometimes. Think of it like this: Would you hold a grudge against a child who was learning to walk and fell down? Of course not! You would help them up, dust them off, and encourage them to try again. You need to offer yourself that same level of compassion and empathy.

Forgiveness is not just a gift you give yourself; it's also a gift you give to others. When you choose to forgive, you break the cycle of pain and resentment. You create space for healing and making amends, not just for yourself, but for those around you. Your act of forgiveness can have a ripple effect, inspiring others to do the same. It can create a more compassionate, more understanding, and more loving world. And isn't that the kind of world we all want to live in?

We can choose to become better versions of ourselves, rising above the pain to create a more positive future. This is the true essence of forgiveness, and it's the best revenge. This path requires courage, vulnerability, and a willingness to confront your pain. But the rewards are immeasurable. As you release the weight of resentment and welcome the freedom of forgiveness, you open yourself up to a life filled with more joy, more peace, and more love.

The Prophet Muhammad (peace be upon him) said,

"Shall I not tell you of a person who is forbidden for the Hellfire and the Hellfire is forbidden for him? Every person who is near (to people), is easy going and soft (in nature)." (Jami' at-Tirmidhi, 2488)

This Hadith suggests that forgiveness and gentleness are qualities that can protect us from harm and lead us to a better place. It's a beautiful reminder that forgiveness is not only beneficial for our emotional well-being but also for our spiritual growth.

So, step onto the bridge of forgiveness, choosing one person for whom you will work on forgiving, whether it's yourself or someone else. This is your first step towards freedom, releasing the chains of the past and welcoming a brighter future. Be patient with yourself, and trust that with each step you take, you are moving closer to healing and peace.

I am enamoured of my own grief and pain,

For it makes me well-pleasing to my peerless King.

~

Chapter 4

THE HAVEN OF COMPASSION

If you desire sanity in this embarrassment,

Stuff not the ear of your mind with cotton.

Take the cotton of evil suggestions from the mind's ear,

That the heavenly voice from above may enter it,

That you may understand that riddle of His,

That you may be cognisant of that open secret.

Then the mind's ear becomes the sensorium of inspiration;

For what is this Divine voice but the inward voice?

– Rumi

Rumi, in these beautiful verses, offers us a roadmap to finding peace within ourselves. He speaks of an "open secret," a wisdom that's available to us all if only we can learn to listen. He talks about "this embarrassment", which is what we often feel when we mess up or fall short of our own expectations. It is in these moments that our inner critic loves to pipe up, filling our minds with harsh judgments and negative thoughts. Rumi likens this to stuffing cotton in the ears of our minds, blocking out the voice of the soul. He urges us to take out that "cotton," to quiet that inner critic, so we can hear a kinder, more supportive voice—the voice of our own inner wisdom, the voice of the Divine within. This chapter focuses on learning to tune into that inner voice, the voice of self-compassion. It's about creating a safe, nurturing space within yourself, a sanctuary where you can find refuge from the storms of self-doubt and criticism. Show yourself the same compassion and kindness you would offer a close friend. By silencing our inner critic, we can create space for self-compassion to flourish, allowing us to heal, grow, and discover the strength and resilience that lie within us.

The Inner Critic

Imam Ali said, "How can you have no pity on yourself as you have on others?" (Nahjul-Balagha, Sermon 221)

This is a powerful question that encourages self-compassion as a form of caring. Many of us, especially those who have experienced trauma or hardship, have a harsh inner critic. It's that voice inside your head that constantly criticizes, judges, and belittles you. It tells you that you're not good enough, that you're a failure, that you don't deserve love or happiness. This inner critic is often a product of past experiences, internalized messages from others, or societal pressures to be perfect.

This voice can be incredibly destructive, eroding your self-esteem, fueling anxiety and depression, and preventing you from taking risks or pursuing your dreams. It's like having a constant bully living inside your head, tearing you down at every opportunity. But here's the thing: that inner critic isn't the real you. It's a distorted reflection, a warped echo of past hurts and negative beliefs. It's not the voice of truth, but rather the voice of fear and insecurity. And just like any bully, it can be silenced. The antidote to the harsh inner critic is self-compassion. It's about treating yourself with the same kindness, understanding, and empathy that you would offer a close friend who was struggling. Recognize that you're human, you're imperfect, and that's okay; you are worthy of love and acceptance, just as you are.

Think about how you would respond to a friend who came to you feeling down on themselves, struggling with self-doubt, or facing a difficult challenge. You would likely offer words of encouragement and support. You would remind them of their strengths, their resilience, and their inherent worth. Self-compassion is about offering that same level of kindness and support to yourself.

Imagine you're learning to ride a bike. You're wobbly and unsure, and you fall a few times. Would you yell at yourself, call yourself stupid, and tell yourself you're never going to get it? Probably not. You'd likely encourage yourself, remind yourself that it takes practice, and maybe even ask for help from someone more experienced. Self-compassion is like being that encouraging voice, that supportive friend, to yourself. It's about realizing that learning and growing takes time, that setbacks are normal, and that you deserve kindness and patience, especially when you're struggling.

Research shows that practicing self-compassion positively impacts our mental and emotional well-being, reducing stress, anxiety, and depression while increasing feelings of happiness, optimism, and resilience. Studies have even shown that self-compassion can change the way our brains function. When we treat ourselves with kindness and empathy, we activate the same neural pathways that are activated when we receive compassion from others. This can help to soothe the nervous system, reduce the production of stress hormones, and promote feelings of calm and well-being.

Exercise

Let's try a self-compassion exercise.

1. **Close your eyes and take a few deep breaths.** Inhale slowly and deeply, filling your lungs with air. Exhale slowly and completely, releasing any tension you might be holding in your body.

2. **Now, bring to mind a recent situation where you struggled or felt inadequate.** Maybe you made a mistake at work, had an argument with a loved

one, or felt disappointed in yourself for not meeting a goal.

3. **Visualize your inner critic's reaction to this situation.** What harsh words or judgments did it hurl at you? What negative beliefs did it reinforce?

4. **Now, imagine a dear friend coming to you with the same struggle, expressing the same pain and self-doubt.** What compassionate words would you **offer** them? How would you comfort and support them?

5. **Write down the compassionate response you would give your friend.** Use kind, **understanding**, and encouraging language. Remind them of their strengths, their resilience, and their inherent worth.

6. **Now, direct that same compassionate response to yourself.** Say those same words to yourself, **either** silently or out loud. Let yourself feel the warmth and kindness of those words.

7. **Place your hand over your heart and take a few more deep breaths.** Feel the gentle pressure of your hand and allow yourself to receive the compassion you've offered yourself.

This is just one example of a self-compassion exercise. The key is to practice regularly and to make it a habit to treat yourself with the same kindness and understanding that you would offer a friend.

Challenging Your Negative Self

The Prophet Muhammad (peace be upon him) stated: **"The believer should not humiliate himself."** (Sunan Ibn Majah, 4016)

One of the most vital parts of self-compassion is learning to challenge your negative self-talk. It's that part of you that whispers doubts, criticizes your every move, and magnifies your flaws. It's a common struggle especially when we're feeling vulnerable or have experienced setbacks. But you don't have to believe everything it says.

Here's the key: that negative self is not the real you. It's a distorted reflection, a collection of learned fears and insecurities. And, most importantly, you have the power to disarm it. Learning to manage this negative self-talk is a crucial part of cultivating self-compassion. Think of it like this: that inner critic is like a frightened part of you, lashing out because it's scared. It's trying to protect you, in its own misguided way, by keeping you from taking risks or facing potential disappointments. But its methods are harsh and unhelpful. Instead of giving in to its negativity, try to approach it with understanding and compassion.

Here's a gentle way to start challenging your negative self-talk:

Become aware of the negative thoughts that are running through your mind. What is your inner critic saying? Ask yourself:

Is this thought really true?

Is there any evidence to support it?

Is there another way of looking at this situation?

What are the common themes and patterns in its messages?

Practice this mindful observation without judgment. It is pivotal to develop this skill. Most often our negative self talks in absolutes, using words like "always," or "never."

Replace the negative thought with a more positive and realistic one. For example, instead of thinking, "I'm such a failure," you could think, "I made a mistake, but I can learn from it and do better next time." Repeat positive statements about yourself, such as "I am strong," "I am capable," "I am worthy of love and respect."

Keep repeating and reinforcing those new, more compassionate statements. Write them down. Say them aloud. Make them your new mantra. The more you practice, the more natural it will feel.

And find comfort in these benevolent words from the Quran:

> **"Allah does not burden a soul beyond that it can bear."**
>
> **(Surah Al-Baqarah, 2:286)**

This verse is a beautiful reminder that we are not given challenges that are beyond our capacity to handle. It's a source of comfort and strength, knowing that we have the inner resources to cope with whatever life throws our way.

You, my friend, are stronger than you think. You have within you the strength and resilience to overcome any challenge, including the challenge of disarming your negative self. Self-compassion is about nurturing that inner strength, about being your own best ally on this journey. It's about reminding yourself, especially when the negative self is at its loudest, that you are capable, you are worthy, and you are deeply loved, by yourself and by the Divine. This is a process of shedding old patterns and nurturing new ones. Be patient with yourself, celebrate your progress, and know that every step you take towards self-compassion is a step towards inner peace and a more fulfilling life.

Distinguishing Self-Compassion from Self-Love and Self-Esteem

It's important to understand that self-compassion is different from self-love and self-esteem. While self-love is about appreciating your strengths and beauty, self-compassion is about tending to your wounds, offering yourself kindness and understanding in the face of pain and difficulty. Self-esteem is often based on external validation and achievements, while self-compassion is about inherent worth and acceptance, regardless of performance or accomplishments.

Self-compassion is not about feeling good about yourself all the time, but being a good friend to yourself, especially when you're feeling bad. Self-love might be something we focus on more in later chapters, as we move towards valuing our true selves. But for now, the focus is on cultivating that inner sanctuary of self-compassion, that safe space where we can find comfort and support, no matter what challenges we face.

Self-compassion is the foundation of inner resilience. When you treat yourself with kindness and compassion, you create a buffer against the inevitable challenges of life. You develop the ability to bounce back from setbacks, to learn from your mistakes, and to keep moving forward, even when things get tough. Think of it like building a house. You wouldn't build a house on a shaky foundation, would you? You would make sure the foundation was strong and solid, able to withstand the weight of the structure and the elements. Self-compassion is the foundation of your emotional well-being. It's the bedrock upon which you can build a life of resilience, strength, and joy.

Cultivating self-compassion benefits not only you but also those around you. When you treat yourself with kindness, you're more likely to treat others with kindness. When you're more forgiving of your own flaws, you're more likely to be forgiving of the flaws of others. Self-compassion creates a ripple effect, spreading outward from you to your relationships, your community, and the world. It's like a pebble dropped into a pond, creating concentric circles that expand outward, touching everything in their path.

Self-compassion and inner resilience are not something you achieve once and then forget about. It's a daily commitment to treating yourself with kindness and respect. There will be times when you stumble, when you fall back into old patterns of self-criticism and negativity. The key is to keep practicing, to keep returning to the principles of self-compassion, and to keep building that inner sanctuary of peace and strength.

Make a commitment to yourself today to practice self-compassion. Start small. Choose one act of kindness you will do for yourself each day this week. It could be something as simple as taking a few deep breaths, repeating a positive affirmation, or writing down three things you appreciate about yourself. The key is to start building that foundation of self-compassion, brick by brick, day by day.

Building a sanctuary within takes time and effort, but it is one of the most rewarding things you can do for yourself. It's about creating a safe haven, a place of refuge, where you can always find comfort, acceptance, and love, no matter what storms may rage around you. And as you cultivate that inner sanctuary, remember Rumi's words:

"Stop acting so small. You are the universe in ecstatic motion."

(Translation by Coleman Barks)

He's telling us to break free from the limitations we place on ourselves and to stop seeing ourselves as small, insignificant, or unworthy. This is what self-compassion is all about. This means recognizing our inherent worth, our capacity for growth, and our ability to heal.

You are not small or insignificant. You are a powerful, resilient, beautiful being, capable of incredible growth and transformation. Welcome that power. Cherish that beauty. Accept yourself with compassion, kindness, and unwavering love.

∼

Chapter 5

OPEN HANDS, OPEN HEART

Watch the face of each one, regard it well,

It may be by serving thou wilt recognize Truth's face.

As there are many demons with men's faces,

It is wrong to join hand with every one.

So vile hypocrites steal the language of Darveshes,

In order to beguile the simple with their trickery.

The works of the righteous are light and heat,

The works of the evil, treachery and shamelessness.

– Rumi

Rumi, in these verses, offers us a wise caution as we navigate the complex world of human connection. He reminds us that not everyone is trustworthy, and that appearances can be deceiving. "Demons with men's faces," he warns, can mislead us with their words and actions. This is especially true when we're rebuilding trust in others. After being hurt, it's natural to be wary, to question who we can truly rely on. This chapter is about learning to discern, to "watch the face of each one" and to look beyond the surface. It's about recognizing that true connection is built on a foundation of honesty and integrity, on actions that align with words, on "light and heat" rather than "treachery and shamelessness." It is a reminder to trust your instincts. As we weave the tapestry of our relationships, we must choose our threads carefully, discerning who is worthy of our trust and who might unravel the delicate fabric we're creating. This doesn't mean becoming cynical or closing ourselves off, but rather approaching connection with both an open heart and a discerning eye, allowing ourselves to be guided by both intuition and observation as we rebuild trust and create meaningful bonds.

Trust forms the foundation of all meaningful relationships, the invisible thread that connects us, creating safety, security, and belonging. But trust is also incredibly fragile. It can be shattered in an instant by a betrayal, a lie, a careless word, or a broken promise. And when that happens, it can feel like the entire fabric of our lives has been torn apart. In this chapter, we'll explore how to rebuild trust, both within ourselves and in our relationships with others. It's about understanding that while trust can be fragile, it can also be rebuilt, stronger and more resilient than before. It's a process of learning to connect, carefully weaving a new tapestry of relationships, thread by thread.

When trust is broken, especially in significant relationships, it can leave deep wounds. It can make us question our judgment, our ability to discern truth from falsehood, and our own worthiness of love and connection. We may become hesitant to open ourselves up to others, fearing that we'll be hurt again. We may build walls around our hearts, isolating ourselves in an attempt to protect ourselves from further pain. It's necessary to acknowledge that rebuilding trust is not an easy process. It takes time, effort, and a willingness to be vulnerable. It requires courage, patience, and a commitment to honesty and open communication. It is work. But it's also one of the most rewarding things we can do, both for ourselves and for our relationships.

The Golden Thread of Trust

Our lives are like an exquisite tapestry, a beautiful and complex work of art woven from many different threads. Each thread represents a relationship, an experience, a connection that you have with the world. Some threads are bright and vibrant, representing joyful and fulfilling relationships. Others are darker, representing painful or difficult experiences. But all of these threads, both the light and the dark, are essential to the overall beauty and complexity of the tapestry. Trust is the golden thread that weaves through the entire tapestry, connecting all the other threads together. It's what gives the tapestry its strength, its resilience, and its ability to withstand the wear and tear of life. When trust is broken, it's as if that golden thread has been cut, leaving a hole in the tapestry. The surrounding threads may become loose, and the overall structure may weaken. But the beauty of a tapestry is that it can be repaired. New threads can be woven in, and the broken threads can be mended. It takes time, patience, and skill, but it is possible to restore the tapestry to its former glory, and even make it stronger and more beautiful than before.

To trust others, you must first learn to trust yourself, which may seem counterintuitive if your judgment has failed you in the past. But the truth is, if you don't trust yourself, it's very difficult to trust anyone else. Trusting yourself means listening to your inner voice, your intuition, and that gut feeling that tells you when something is right or wrong. It means honoring your own needs and boundaries, even when it's difficult. It means believing in your own worthiness and your ability to make good decisions.

Boundaries: The Framework of Trust

Boundaries are essential to building trust acting as the framework of a tapestry, providing structure and support for the threads to be woven upon. Boundaries define what you are and are not comfortable with, what you will and will not tolerate, and what you need in order to feel safe and respected in a relationship. They are not about controlling others, but about taking care of yourself.

When you set healthy boundaries, you are communicating to others that you value yourself and that you expect to be treated with respect. This, in turn, creates a foundation of trust and mutual respect in your relationships.

Here are a few steps to help you rebuild trust in yourself:

Acknowledge your past mistakes. We all make mistakes. It's part of being human. Instead of beating yourself up over past errors in judgment, acknowledge them, learn from them, and forgive yourself as we have learned in previous chapters.

Pay attention to your gut feelings and inner voice. Your intuition is a powerful guide, and the more you listen to it, the stronger it becomes.

Learn to identify and prioritize your own needs. Don't be afraid to ask for what you need, and what you don't, even if it means saying no to others.

Acknowledge and celebrate your accomplishments, no matter how small. This will help you build confidence in your own abilities and judgment. When you make a commitment to yourself, follow through. This builds self-trust and reinforces the belief that you are reliable and trustworthy.

The Quran says,

> **"O you who have believed, do not betray Allah and the Messenger, nor betray your trusts while you know."**
> **(Surah Al-Anfal, 8:27)**

This verse emphasizes the importance of trust, both in our relationship with the Divine and in our relationships with others. It reminds us that trust is a sacred responsibility and we should strive to be worthy of the trust that others place in us.

Be Vulnerable

Vulnerability is often seen as a weakness, but in reality, it's a strength. It is not about oversharing or spilling your guts to everyone you meet. It takes courage to be vulnerable, to let down your guard, and to show your true self to others. But it's also the key to authentic connection. When you allow yourself to be vulnerable, you create space for deeper intimacy and understanding in your relationships. You welcome others to see, know, and love you completely and honestly, with all your imperfections. This means being honest and authentic in your interactions, about sharing your true thoughts and feelings with those you trust. It's about taking a risk.

Imagine holding a precious jewel in your hand. You can keep it hidden away, safe from harm, but no one will ever see its beauty. Or you can open your hand and share it with the world, knowing that there's a risk it might get scratched or even broken, but also knowing that its beauty will shine even brighter when shared. Vulnerability is like opening your hand and sharing that precious jewel with others. It's a risk, but it's also an invitation to connect with others, to open your heart to love, and to let that love reshape your life into something beautiful, filled with joy and wonder.

Mending the Tapestry of Trust

Learning to trust again after a betrayal can be a daunting task. It's like learning to swim after nearly drowning. You're hesitant to get back in the water, fearing that you'll be pulled under again. But it's important to remember that not all people are the same. Just because one person betrayed your trust doesn't mean everyone will do the same. It's easy to generalize based on one negative experience, but it's not fair to assume that everyone is like that. People are individuals with their own values and principles. There are trustworthy people in the world, people who are deserving of your trust. It's essential to give others a chance and not let one person's actions taint your perception of others. Trust is a delicate thing, but it's worth taking the risk to build it with the right people who deserve it. The key is learning to discern who those people are.

When assessing trustworthiness, look for these traits:

❖ Do their words and actions align?

❖ Do they follow through on their commitments?

❖ Do they show genuine concern for your feelings and well-being?

❖ Can they put themselves in your shoes?

❖ Do they respect your boundaries, even when they don't agree with them?

❖ Are they truthful, even if it's difficult?

- ❖ Do they own up to their mistakes?

- ❖ Do they take responsibility for their actions?

- ❖ Are they willing to make amends when they've hurt you?

- ❖ Are they willing to communicate openly and honestly with you, even about difficult topics?

- ❖ Are they willing to be transparent and share information with you, or do they keep secrets and hide things?

It's also important to pay attention to your own intuition. If something feels off, it probably is. Don't ignore those inner nudges. They are there to guide you.

The Prophet Muhammad (peace be upon him) advised,

"A believer is not stung twice from the same hole." - (Sunan Abi Dawud, 4862)

This Hadith is often interpreted as a warning to learn from our mistakes and to be cautious about trusting those who have betrayed us in the past. It doesn't mean that we should never trust again, but that we should be wise in our choices and pay attention to the signs.

Exercise

This week, choose one relationship where you will take a risk and be vulnerable by showing your true self. This could be sharing a feeling you've been holding back, expressing a need you've been afraid to voice, or simply letting your guard down a little bit more than usual. Vulnerability is the key to deeper connection.

Rebuilding trust after it's been broken is a delicate process. It requires both parties to be willing to put in the work, to be honest, and to be patient. It's not something that can be rushed or forced.

If you're the one who broke the trust, it's indispensable to acknowledge the pain you caused, take responsibility for your actions, and make amends. You need to demonstrate through your actions that you are committed to changing your behavior and rebuilding the relationship.

If you're the one who was betrayed, it's vital to allow yourself time to heal. Don't feel pressured to forgive or reconcile before you're ready. You need to process your emotions, set clear boundaries, and identify what will make you feel safe and secure in the relationship again.

Imam Ali stated,

"Faith (the intention in your heart) is the criterion of your deeds; 'taqwa' (abstaining from sins and disobedience) is your shield and protector; good manners are your adornment, and forbearance is the fortress of your honor." (Nahjul-Balagha).

Imam Ali's words taught us that the foundation of this path resides within our hearts, in the sincerity of our intentions. Let your actions be guided by 'taqwa', a conscious awareness of your responsibilities, and a commitment to acting with honesty and respect.

When we weave our lives together, connecting authentically, heart to heart, we create something far more beautiful and enduring than anything we could create alone. It's about choosing to see the light in others, even after having known darkness. It's about the courage to open ourselves to vulnerability, even when fear whispers warnings. It's about choosing love, even if it demands the difficult work of forgiveness and understanding.

Mind you, it is not a neat, tidy process with a clear beginning, middle, and end. It's more like a winding road, with twists and turns, hills and valleys, and sometimes even a few detours. There will be moments of clarity and connection, and there will be moments of doubt and fear. The main thing is to keep moving forward, one step at a time. You are not simply rebuilding an old tapestry, you are weaving a new one. A tapestry that is stronger, more resilient, and more beautiful than the one before. A tapestry that reflects the lessons you've learned, the growth you've experienced, and the love you've chosen to welcome. Every thread in the tapestry is connected to every other thread. Every act of trust, every moment of vulnerability, every expression of love sends ripples throughout the entire tapestry, strengthening the connections between us all.

As we learn to trust again, to love again, to connect again, we create a more beautiful and compassionate world for ourselves and for generations to come. Find your way to express the love that resides within you. Trust your intuition, honor your boundaries, and allow yourself to be guided by the wisdom of your heart. You are a vital part of this intricate and interconnected web of life. Your choices, your actions, your willingness to trust and love matter. They make a difference, not only in your own life but in the lives of everyone you touch. **Your light is needed. Let it shine.**

~

Chapter 6

THE PHOENIX RISES

When a master places a spade in the hand of a slave,

The slave knows his meaning without being told.

Like this spade, our hands are our Master's hints to us;

Yea, if ye consider, they are His directions to us.

When ye have taken to heart His hints,

Ye will shape your life in reliance on their direction;

Wherefore these hints disclose His intent,

Take the burden from you, and appoint your work.

He that bears it makes it bearable by you,

He that is able makes it within your ability.

Accept His command, and you will be able to execute it;

Seek union with Him, and you will find yourselves united.

– Rumi

In these luminous verses, Rumi unveils a sacred truth: our journey through life is not aimless, but divinely guided by signs we must learn to recognize. Like the slave who understands the master's purpose simply by the tool placed in his hand, we too are given "hints," subtle nudges from the Divine, directing us toward our true path. This chapter explores how to identify those quiet nudges and intuitions that guide our hearts. It's about comprehending that the challenges we've faced, the wounds we've healed, the tears we've shed, the forgiveness we've offered, the self-compassion we've cultivated, and the trust we've rebuilt—all of these have been preparing us for this moment, shaping us into the people we were meant to be.

Now, as you stand on the threshold of wholeness, honoring your core identity, know that you are not alone. You are being guided, supported, and empowered to step fully into your authentic power and to live a life that is aligned with your deepest values and highest purpose. The path that brought you here, has strengthened you, and now, as you value your true self, you have all you need within you to live a life of meaning, purpose, and joy. Trust in the journey, grasp the hints, and step boldly into the magnificent tapestry of your life, knowing that you are a valuable and beautiful thread in the grand design, a masterpiece in the making. Your time to shine has arrived.

"This being human is a guest house. Every morning a new arrival. A joy, a depression, a meanness, some momentary awareness comes as an unexpected visitor. Welcome and entertain them all! Even if they are a crowd of sorrows, who violently sweep your house empty of its furniture, still, treat each guest honorably. He may be clearing you out for some new delight."

Rumi (Translation by Coleman Barks)

Rumi's words offer a powerful metaphor for the human experience, inviting us to see our lives as a "guest house," and our emotions, thoughts, and experiences as "visitors." Some visitors are pleasant, bringing joy and happiness. Others are difficult, bringing pain, sorrow, or anger. But Rumi suggests that we welcome them all, even the unpleasant ones, for they all have something to teach us. This is the essence of valuing your authentic self. This involves acknowledging and accepting all parts of yourself, the light and the dark, the joyful and the painful, the beautiful and the messy. It's about realizing that every experience, every emotion, every thought, has shaped you into the unique and complex individual you are today. This chapter is about coming home to yourself. It's about integrating all the pieces of your experience—the wounds, the tears, the forgiveness, the self-compassion, the trust—into a beautiful whole.

The Mosaic of Wholeness

When we experience trauma, loss, or deep disappointment, it can feel like we've been shattered into a million pieces. We may feel fragmented, disconnected, and lost, unsure of who we are or how we fit into the world anymore. This feeling of fragmentation is a natural response to pain. It's a way of coping with experiences that are too overwhelming to process all at once. But here's the truth: you may be broken into several pieces, but you are not beyond repair.

Think of a mosaic. It's made up of many pieces, some bright and colorful, others dark and muted. Some pieces are smooth and polished, others are rough and jagged. But it's the combination of all these different pieces that creates the beauty of the whole. Your life is like that mosaic. You are not merely a collection of shattered fragments, but a work of art in progress. Each piece, each experience, each wound, each triumph, is a part of the whole. It's made up of diverse experiences, some joyful, some painful, some easy, some difficult. But it's the totality of those experiences that makes you who you are. You're not broken; you're beautifully whole, and your soul's truth is waiting to be discovered, cherished, and celebrated.

One of the most valuable steps towards wholeness is integrating your past experiences. It means acknowledging what happened, accepting the impact it had on you, and finding a way to incorporate those experiences into your present life in a healthy and meaningful way. Your bad experiences are part of the fabric of your life. But you can choose how you weave them into the overall design. You can choose to focus on the beauty of the whole tapestry, rather than getting lost in the darkness of individual threads.

Give yourself permission to acknowledge what happened to you, without judgment or shame. Your story is your story, and it deserves to be heard, even if only by you. Allow yourself to feel the full range of emotions associated with your hurtful experiences. Don't try to suppress or avoid them. Feel them, name them, and let them move through you. Identify any negative beliefs about yourself or the world that arose from your experiences. Challenge those beliefs with evidence from your present life. Are they really true? Look for the lessons you've learned, the strength you've gained, and the ways in which your experiences have shaped you into the person you are today. Treat yourself with kindness and respect as you navigate this process. Healing takes time and it's okay to ask for help. Connect with a therapist, counselor, or support group to help you process your experiences and develop healthy coping mechanisms.

Integrating the Past: A Reflection

1. **Find a quiet space where you can sit comfortably without distractions.** Close your eyes if it feels comfortable, and take a few deep breaths.

2. **Think about an experience that has been challenging for you.** Don't choose the most painful one, but something you feel ready to explore.

3. **Acknowledge the experience without judgment.** Simply observe it as a fact, a part of your **story.**

4. **What emotions come up when you think about this experience?** Name them, and allow yourself to feel them fully.

5. **What beliefs about yourself or the world did you form because of this experience?** Are those beliefs still serving you?

6. **Now, think about the lessons you've learned from this experience.** How has it made you stronger, wiser, or more compassionate?

7. **How can you integrate this experience into your life in a healthy way?** Can you use it to help others? Can you draw strength from it?

8. **Take a few more deep breaths, and thank yourself for having the courage to explore your past.**

As you begin to integrate your past moments, you'll start to discover your inner essence, the self that existed before the trauma, before the disappointments, before the pain. This is the self that is whole, complete, and inherently worthy of love and belonging.

Exercise

Discovering your core identity is like peeling back the layers of an onion, each layer represents a different aspect of your personality, your beliefs, your values, and your experiences. Some layers may be beautiful and lively, others may be dark and painful. But they are all part of who you are. This exercise is about getting to know yourself on a deeper level, knowing what makes you tick, what brings you joy, and what you truly value. It is a practice you can incorporate into your daily routine.

1. **When have you felt most passionate?** Think about moments when you felt fully engaged, energized, and alive. What were you doing? Who were you with? What about those experiences made you feel that way?

2. **When have you felt most powerful?** This isn't about power over others, but about feeling confident, capable, and in control of your own life. What were **the** circumstances? What strengths did you draw upon?

3. **What makes your heart sing?** What activities, people, or places bring you the most joy and fulfillment? What makes you lose track of time?

4. **Write about those experiences in detail.** Describe the sights, sounds, smells, and emotions associated with them. Let yourself relive those moments on the page.

As you explore these questions, you'll begin to uncover the unique gifts and talents that you have to offer the world. You'll start to see yourself not as a broken, fragmented being, but as a whole, complete, and beautiful individual, with a unique purpose and a powerful story to tell.

The Quran offers us a hint from the Divine,

"Did He not find you unguided then guided you?"

(Ad-Duhaa, 93:7)

This verse speaks to the inherent human capacity for growth, transformation, and finding our way back to our true selves, even when we feel lost or broken. It suggests that guidance is always available to us if we are open to receiving it.

Here are some ways to start living more authentically:

❖ What are the principles that guide your life? What is most important to you? Learn to say no to things that don't align with your values or your priorities. Protect your time, energy, and emotional well-being.

❖ Find healthy outlets for your emotions and your creativity. This could be through writing, painting, music, dance, or any other form of artistic expression. What lights you up? What makes you feel alive? Make time for the activities that bring you joy and fulfillment.

❖ Surround yourself with people who support and encourage you to be your true self. Share your thoughts and feelings honestly and openly, even if it's difficult. Nobody is perfect. Accept your flaws and imperfections as part of what makes you unique and beautiful. Learn to love and accept yourself, just as you are, in this moment.

Once you begin to discover your true self, the next step is to start living authentically, to express yourself fully and honestly in the world. This means aligning your actions with your values, pursuing your passions, and sharing your gifts with others. It's like finding your voice after years of silence. It's about speaking your truth, even when it's difficult, even if it's unpopular. It's about daring to be seen, to be heard, to be known for who you truly are.

Living authentically and valuing your core identity transforms not only your life but also inspires others to do the same, creating a ripple effect, spreading light, love, and authenticity throughout the world. Your authenticity, your courage, and your willingness to be vulnerable can have a significant effect. It can inspire others to step into their own truth, to welcome their own imperfections, and to live more fulfilling lives. This is the power of honoring your true self. It's not just about personal transformation, but also making a difference in the world. It's about being a beacon of light, a source of inspiration, a catalyst for positive change.

The Prophet Muhammad (peace be upon him) said,

"The most beloved people to Allah are those who are most beneficial to people." (Al-Mu'jam al-Awsat, 6192)

This Hadith highlights the importance of living a life of service, of using our gifts and talents to make a positive impact on the world. When we value our true selves and live authentically, we are better able to fulfill this purpose.

My friend, the journey to wholeness, to truly honoring who you are, is before you now. It is a path of continuous growth, learning, and rediscovering who you are at your core. And you don't have to have it all figured out right now. Start where you are. This is your invitation to take one small step today, a single action that feels true to you, that brings you joy, that aligns with your values. Maybe it's picking up that paintbrush again, or maybe it's finally having that honest conversation. Whatever it is, let it be a step toward a more authentic and fulfilling life.

Welcome the imperfections along the way, let your past inform you, and step into your genuine being. This path to wholeness is where you'll find unfathomable joy and lasting fulfillment. You're not alone; we're all traveling on this path together, learning and growing, supporting one another. You are a unique and beautiful soul, with a story to tell and a light to share with the world. Welcome it all, my friend, and let that light shine brightly.

Accept His command, and you will be able to execute it;

Seek union with Him, and you will find yourselves united.

· · ·◦· ·●·•~· • · ·

From Here Onward

My dear friend, before we conclude, let's be clear: your feelings and experiences are genuine and matter deeply. The pain, the anger, the fear—they are all a part of your story, but they are not the end of it. Acknowledge them, honor them, for they have shaped you. But seriously, you're more than that.

The fact that you're here, seeking a way forward, reading these words, shows incredible strength. You've already taken steps that many are afraid to even face. You've looked into the shadows of your past, and that takes immense courage. Remember that bravery. Hold onto it. You've already come so far, and that resilience will continue to carry you forward. Your past has shaped you, yes, but you have the power to decide who you want to be moving forward. Every day, every moment, is a new opportunity to make a choice, to choose to heal, to choose hope, to choose the life you want to live.

Imagine a life where you wake up with hope, where relationships feel safe and supportive, and where you feel at peace with yourself, where joy is not a fleeting visitor but a constant companion. This is possible, but it won't happen overnight, and it won't always be easy. But with each small, consistent step, you'll move closer to that vision.

You don't need to face this by yourself alone; you've got support. Surrounding yourself with people who uplift you can make all the difference. Whether it's a friend, a family member, a support group, a therapist, or even a pet, connection heals. Lean on those who offer you love and support, and allow them to be a source of strength on your journey.

Don't ever forget this: you are worthy of happiness and love, simply because you exist. Nothing you've been through, no mistake you've made, no challenge you faced, takes away your inherent value. You deserve a life filled with joy, purpose, and authentic connection.

So, as you close this book, I leave you with a simple, yet powerful, call to action: today, take a moment to do something that makes you smile. Whether it's listening to a favorite song, stepping outside to feel the sun on your face, calling a loved one, reading a beloved poem by Rumi, or simply taking a few deep breaths, do something that brings you joy. You deserve it. And keep doing it, every day. Make it a practice, a ritual, a reminder that joy is not a luxury but a necessity, especially in the process of healing.

This is a new beginning, my friend. Welcome it with courage, with hope, and with an unwavering belief in your own capacity to heal and thrive. The world needs your light, your unique perspective, and your beautiful, resilient spirit. May your path be filled with peace, with love, and with the knowing that you are whole, you are loved, and you are meant to shine.

- Ahmed Mustafa

About the Author

Hello, my name is Ahmed Mustafa, and like many of you, I'm just a regular person trying to navigate this complex world we live in. I've never considered myself a scholar or an expert, but rather a curious explorer on a journey to understand life a little better.

We live in a time that's incredibly fast-paced and competitive. Everywhere we look, we're encouraged to strive for individual success, to climb the ladder, and to achieve more. It's easy to get caught up in this race, focusing on what we can achieve for ourselves. But during all this striving, I started to notice a disconnect. I realized that despite all the advancements and opportunities around us, many of us still feel a sense of unease, a feeling that something is missing.

What I've come to understand is that despite the competitive landscape of modern society, our core human desires remain the same. We all long for **connection**; to feel loved, understood, and part of something bigger than ourselves. We crave **purpose**; a sense that our lives have meaning and that we're contributing to the world in some way. We seek **security**;

not just financial stability, but also emotional and mental well-being, a feeling of safety and peace within ourselves. And we're constantly searching for a **balance**; a way to pursue our individual dreams while also fulfilling our responsibilities to our families, communities, and the world around us.

These desires, these deep-seated longings, highlight the ongoing struggle many of us face. We live in a world that often prioritizes individual success over communal well-being, and finding our place in it can feel like trying to solve a complicated puzzle. How can we be successful and also be fulfilled? How can we take care of ourselves and also take care of others?

My journey led me to the **wisdom of the East**, particularly the teachings of Rumi and the principles found within Islam. These ancient teachings, though born in a different time and place, resonated deeply with the questions I was asking about modern life. I discovered that they offered thoughtful insights into the human condition, providing guidance on how to find inner peace, heal from past hurts, and build meaningful relationships; the very things that many of us are searching for today.

I'm not here to tell you that I have all the answers. But what I can share is my own exploration of these eternal principles and how they've helped me to better understand myself and the world around me. The books I've written are a reflection of this journey. They are an attempt to bridge the gap between ancient wisdom and modern challenges, to show how the teachings of the East can offer practical solutions to the problems we face in our everyday lives.

My hope is that through these books, you'll find tools and insights that echo with your own experiences, that you'll discover a path towards greater peace, purpose, and connection, and eventually, together, we can create a world that values not just individual success, but also the well-being of us all. Because at the end of the day, we're all in this together, searching for a way to live a life that is both meaningful and fulfilling.

· · ·⌒· ·●· ·∼· · ·

Explore Other
Rumi-Inspired Books

ISBN: 978-1-998843-46-6

ISBN: 978-1-998843-52-7